PATRIOT HILL

A SOLDIER'S STORY

Elbert Hill

ISBN 979-8-88644-761-3 (Paperback)
ISBN 979-8-88644-762-0 (Digital)

Covenant Books
11661 Hwy 707
Murrells Inlet, SC 29576
www.covenantbooks.com

ACKNOWLEDGMENTS

I would like to pay my respects to all the veterans of America and their families who supported them while in the United States military. The service that they gave should not go unrewarded and never be forgotten. To the many who chose to serve in times of conflict and to all those who served during peacetime situations. From the time of the Revolutionary War and wars thereafter, the people of the United States of America have supported their country and answered the call to military duty.

Those who are fortunate enough not to endure the magnitude of war may sometimes take for granted their freedom and the American way of life. There is not a single person who likes the sound of war drums, but sometimes, there is only the course of the war. The preservation of our children and the foundation of our nation must be protected at all costs. This was the determining factor of my military enlistment in 1966.

There was a war in Vietnam and it was a tough time for Black males socially. I still chose to answer the call of military duty. America was my home, and I chose to help protect it. I knew one day I would be like my ancestors before me—raise my family in freedom and peace. It was a difficult choice to make for a young Black male. With hatred groups like the Ku Klux Klan, I pondered over my decision. Even with the prejudice levels in the United States, I decided to enlist. In the words of Abraham Lincoln, a nation divided cannot stand. I felt that I should help defend America.

Once again, the words of President Lincoln came to my mind. He said that America could only be destroyed from within. Working together, we can up whole the American way of life. Perhaps he meant hating other races would cause the eventual collapse of the system.

People working together militarily and in other ways can preserve the American way of life.

The veterans of foreign wars and all conflicts merit care after wars. They are looked upon by younger generations and must be cared for after wars. It would be devastating for future enlistees. This would cause a lower number of troops and national defense problems. Let us not forget events like Veterans' Day. It is more than flying flags and celebrations. It is to remember those who served and died in the line of duty. It is to give appreciation to the people who militarily served America.

We must remember our veterans of various wars. Old soldiers never die; they slowly fade away. I salute my fellow veterans of the present and past and those who are yet to come. If not for the service given by veterans of the past and present, the United States of America could not and would not exist. It is vital for any country to always maintain a strong military at all costs. Without a strong military presence, any nation could perish.

It is the dedication of its citizens that help and maintain the very foundation of any nation. From the days of early history until the present time, nations have always depended on their military to protect and preserve their boundaries. The right to live in a nation of peace is desired by all nations. War is a thing not desired by most of humankind, but at times, it is necessary for the survival of any nation.

With that in mind, a country must have and maintain a strong military presence. It is not a thing that is mandatory, but one that might favor a nation militarily strong. Throughout history, wars have taken place, and a nation's military was called to defend it. We have learned from historical events of war of different nations' survival because of having a strong and mighty military. From these historical events, we gather information on a nation's military survival. We can view which nations existed longer and which did not.

It is extremely expensive to maintain a strong and efficient military, but it is worth the cost and effort. The United States of America is blessed to keep and maintain its military—a military that has stood and preserved our nation for centuries. Let all its citizens be thankful for its presence.

INTRODUCTION

The story you are about to read is a true story. It is a story about an American boy who grew up to become an American soldier. It is filled with events that took place in the life of a Black American male. *Patriot Hill* also tells of the conditions, socially and militarily, during the early nineteen sixties and nineteen seventies. It was a time of social change within the United States of America. There were changes taking place racially and culture wise. These changes, as well as the Vietnam War during the nineteen sixties and seventies, would eventually alter the ways of everyday life in America.

Patriot Hill is a personal story of myself, Elbert Hill Jr. It can also represent the feelings of thousands of other veterans within our country. Within this story, I seek to give an overall view of the Black American veteran's mental and physical traumas, and all other nationalities of war veterans as well. *Patriot Hill* is a story of my life and many historical events. It is a story that tells why the choice was made by an American boy to go to war.

   * ★ *

CHAPTER 1

The Innocence

I was born the second child of three. My parents, Elbert and Lillie Mae Hill, raised us in the state of Louisiana. It was a challenging time for Black people job wise and racially. In the younger years of my life, I did not realize my time of innocence then. My parents married at an incredibly youthful age. The responsibility of having three children weighed heavily on them. Having three children placed more responsibilities on them.

My sister, Barbara was the first born. I was the second born, and my sister, Diane, the third. My father worked hard in a lumber mill in Homer, Louisiana. It was not enough salary to sustain our family financially. My father often talked about leaving the state of Louisiana. He was contemplating a trip to the state of California. He constantly talked to my mother about the financial opportunities in California. Relocating did not set well with my mother. She was just a young woman still in her teens and not used to traveling far.

The seasons turned into years; my mother finally agreed with my dad. They both decided it was best for the family. In the year 1950, they both left the state of Louisiana for California. My parents arranged for my grandparents to care for us while they lived and worked in Los Angeles, California. It is never easy for a family to separate under such conditions. We missed them very much and longed for their presence. Little did we know they were only making a better life financially and in other ways for us.

We learned many different things while staying with my grandparents. We learned to do various chores. It was truly a unique experience. We did chores like feeding the hogs and the chickens. My grandfather would take us hunting on occasion. One of the things I did not like was getting chicken for dinner. Before the chicken was ready for dinner, you had to break the chicken's neck. I did not like that part. I had to chase the chicken around the farmyard quite a lot. It was like running in a track meet and relay. These truly were days of innocence and childhood wonder.

The school we attended was far from our farmhouse. We had to travel a great distance to arrive. We played along the way and ate wild berries along the roadside. After school, we walked home and prepared for dinner. My grandmother treated each one of us with respect and love. She made things like homemade lemonade and homemade ice cream. The food she made was more than good, and we were happy country pumpkins.

Several years had passed since my parents' departure. In the year 1955, my parents came back to Louisiana. They had made trips back previously to visit us, but this time, it was not just to visit us. They had worked hard in Los Angeles, California, and made enough money to help relocate their children. It was a delightful day for us to see them again but made us sad to leave our grandparents.

Our ma and pa had been so good to us through the years. We all broke down in tears as they hugged us goodbye. My father's skills as a sawmill worker had paid off. He had acquired a good-paying job in the furniture manufacturing industry. My parents had lived in a small trailer behind my mother's sister's house in Los Angeles, California. My parents had made enough money to purchase a small home in the South-Central Los Angeles, California, area.

The trip to California was a joyful one. We traveled by train and enjoyed the many sites along the way. The Caucasian people on the train were genuinely nice to us in every way. In Louisiana, we as children feared the laws of Jim Crow and some Caucasian people. I had been taught by my grandmother to honor the signs of Jim Crow.

What happened in a market one time was an unforgettable experience. I became thirsty and saw a water fountain at the rear of the store. There were two water fountains with two signs on them. One said "whites only" and the other "niggers only." The one for whites had cold ice water on the side of it. The one with the nigger sign had mud and looked disgusting. I chose the one for whites and felt a hand pull my head up from the water fountain. It was my grandmother with a scared voice. She said, "Junior, do not drink from that fountain. It will mean trouble." After that, I had a better understanding of the laws of Jim Crow toward Black people.

As a child, I could not believe people could think in such a way. On the way home, I cried and hugged my grandmother in fear. After arriving in Los Angeles, California, we were overjoyed. My parents had decided for us to live around South Central Los Angeles, California. They purchased a home and enrolled me and my two sisters in elementary school. It was terribly interesting to live in our new community and attend the elementary school in Los Angeles, California.

We had the opportunity to live and play with other children and people not of our race. This was different from the life we had in the state of Louisiana. We genuinely enjoyed the years of growing up in our new community. The years passed and we grew up from small children to young adults. The educational system in Los Angeles, California, was particularly good. My older sister, Barbara, was a valedictorian in her junior and high school years. We all graduated from high school.

During my high school days, I was a member of the gymnastics team and a two-year varsity athlete. I enjoyed the sport of gymnastics very much. The years of innocence past once again. As a child, I loved the art of acting and singing. Before my graduation in 1965, I had joined a male singing group. The group was called The Inspirations. We appeared in talent shows and many auditions. We were young and were not aware of the many copyright obstacles. We were appearing at nightclubs in Hollywood, California, and the owner liked our sound. He asked us to come back to his office to record the song. We told him yes and recorded our song for him.

Months passed, and we heard nothing from the nightclub owner. I was sitting in my room one night reading. My older sister, Barbara, knocked on my bedroom door screaming. I opened the door and she screamed out, "Your song is on the radio!" As I listened to the song on the radio, I knew it was ours. The tempo was a bit different, but the beat and lyrics were the same. I talked to my group members, and they had heard it too. After that, the group was not the same. We all drifted our separate ways. We all had our dreams of being great entertainers, but our dreams had broken apart.

In 1965, I began to job hunt. After searching for jobs daily and not finding one, I often thought of the times I did not have to worry about any type of job. My parents took care of all the bills and I was content. I now felt the responsibilities of a young adult and Black man. After many weeks of searching for employment, I got a response. The Southern California Gas Company called me for an interview. This was a moment of completion in every respect. I prepared myself for the interview and prayed as well. The interview went very well and I was hired. I worked and made enough money to pay my parents a small portion of the rent. I also managed to buy a nice mustang car and other necessities.

The job at the gas company was a particularly excellent job. The pay was good, but I desired something different. My parents told me to keep the job at the gas company and its security. I decided to seek employment at a company called Industrial Wire Company. The company made various products of steel and iron rods. It was a very technical-level job. I was a machine-bending rod specialist. The rods had to be bent to a certain degree. It was truly an interesting job. It was a time of social change in America.

I constantly read about the Vietnam War and our involvement. I had never witnessed such things as these before. The days of my childhood innocence had passed. The time for me to face the responsibilities of an adult had come. Thanks to the teachings of my parents and teachings from schools, I was ready to face the world on my own. I decided to leave Industrial Wire Company and prepare for my next move.

* ⭐ *

CHAPTER 2

The Day of Independence

There comes a time in everyone's life to leave their home. It is something that eventually must happen. I had often thought of the time I had to leave home. I was ready to do so, but in no particular hurry to do so. I started dating different girls, and my hormones were running wild. At the age of eighteen, I took a girl on a date and decided to bring her back to my parents' house. I knew that this was wrong, and so did she.

I was raised to respect our house and family members. I had committed the ultimate sin and disrespect toward my family. With my hormones accelerating nonstop with sexual desire, I had sex with her in my bedroom. With our hormones rising, we could not stop. My sexual desires had been satisfied, but the disrespect toward my family was degrading. I felt that I had made too much noise during my activities, and I was right.

The next morning, my father addressed me concerning the issue. He told me of the sounds he had heard coming from my bedroom. I sadly lowered my head and could not speak for several moments. He told me of the disrespect toward the family and house. He also discussed the possibility of me getting a place of my own to stay. Once again, my childhood innocence had dissolved. I was now a young man and ready for my day of independence.

In 1965, I moved out of my parents' house. I found an apartment close to my parents' house, and I often visited them. It was rough going during that time. It was always good to come home to visit. I really missed my mom's cooking and my family. I was working, but very dissatisfied at the time. I had many thoughts about joining the military and leaving home.

As a child, I learned about the United States of America. I grew up to understand the freedom we maintain and love. I was the only male child and did not have to serve in the military, but I truly considered enlisting. Many things happened in the year 1965. As the year changed, so did I.

In early 1966, I was working a job at Industrial Wire Company. I returned from work one day and got a call from my mother. My mother told me that I received a letter from the military. It was a letter from the draft board. I quickly made my way to my mother's house. I read the letter and all it contained.

It was an induction letter from the United States Army. In the year 1966, I prepared for an induction physical examination. The days passed and I anticipated the physical exam. The day finally came, and I made tracks for the induction center in downtown Los Angeles, California.

While in the induction center, I waited patiently. There were hundreds of men my age getting physical exams. My turn came to be examined, and I was ready. After a battery of test papers and physicals, I was sent to the waiting area. I sat there for hours waiting for the results of the examinations and tests. Finally, a military officer notified me about the results. I passed, and I immediately called my parents to let them know.

* ★ *

CHAPTER 3

Basic Training

Many things went through my mind prior to my leaving for the basic training army camp. In the early summer of 1966, I departed for my military basic training camp at Fort Ord, California. Many things went through my mind about my leaving home and where I was headed. As I rode along the California coastline, stars shone brightly that night. I fell asleep thinking of home. The next morning, the bus full of new army recruits arrived at its destination.

We arrived at Fort Ord, California ready for military orientation. We were all given military identification. The new recruits and I were assigned different barracks. We were also taken to the military barber for haircuts. Everything was done in a completely organized fashion. We were sent back to our different barracks and told to rest until the next day.

The next day came exceedingly early with the sound of a trumpet entering the entire barracks. An army officer yelled out the words, "Hit the floor!" All new recruits rose from their beds shivering from the cold and sleepiness. This was the first day of real military life for all of us. The day was filled with many tasks and supply orders. We had to fill orders for clothes and other supplies.

The wake-up call was five o'clock in the morning and we were exhausted. The upcoming days were filled with physical exercise and military discipline. A few weeks later, we began to train on hand-to-hand combat and the use of military weaponry. I became an infantry soldier. The weeks passed, and the training got more intense. Some of the new draftees were falling behind in training. Some even refused to take orders and received a court martial. It was difficult for me to watch it happen to people I knew. The physical and mental training was extremely rough. Never in my entire life had I experienced such physical and mental pressure. If you did not follow orders, you could end up peeling tons of potatoes for the military kitchen. It was a tremendous strain on me both mentally and physically, but I managed to adapt. I had my share of peeling potatoes, but I never received a court martial.

The training grew more advanced as the weeks went by. All soldiers had to be trained on several types of weaponry. We trained on firing automatic weapons and bazooka guns, and entering a gas chamber. Once in the gas chamber, you had to remove your mask. This was mandatory and required by military law. The mask was only off for a few seconds, but caused mild burns to the face and surrounding areas.

After weeks of intense training, my family made a visit to see me. My sister, Barbara asked about my face. I told her about the gas test and she broke down in tears. It was good to see my family and listen to the loving things they had to say. As I sat with them and talked about the happy times at home, I started to think of the days ahead and what might lie ahead for me in the future.

Basic training was ending, and the time to leave for home leave was coming near again. It was time to return home.

CHAPTER 4

Advanced Infantry Training

Upon returning home, I noticed how the neighborhood had changed. It seemed that all the people I once knew were busy with daily activities and social worries about the harsh treatment of Black people by the Los Angeles Police Department. Things were bad when I departed from home to the military, but they seem to have gotten worse during my time away.

I first went to visit my girlfriend at her parents' home. She was glad to see me and told me how good I looked in my uniform. We sat in the living room of their house talking and laughing about different things. We listened to some dance tunes, hugged, and kissed. These were truly moments that I had longed for during basic training. We also talked about my time in the army and her waiting for me. She said that she would wait for me and then marry me upon my military release.

While we danced to slow tunes and soft music, I did not realize that things in the future would alter my life course. We never know what course our lives will take. We can only live for the present and maintain positive thoughts toward the future. I spent several weeks on leave from the military and enjoyed every day of it. The time was coming for me to return to the military for the second half of military training. Three days before I left for the second half of my military training, my parents and sister wanted to give me a going-away party. My going-away party was one to be remembered. Many of my friends and neighbors came to say goodbye.

A few days later, I departed for my advanced infantry training. I had been assigned to a military base in the state of Oklahoma. The military base was called Fort Sill Artillery Training. It specialized in training soldiers to use cannons and heavy artillery. I was proud to be a member of such an elite group of military soldiers. The days at Fort Sill were much like those at Fort Ord. The physical condition and gunnery testing were quit demanding. Within a brief time, I learned to maintain cannon gun fire and drive tanks. It was extremely dangerous work, and accuracy was necessary. One could be killed if the wrong calculations were given.

During my training at Fort Sill, I would sometimes go to the small bars around the fort. Many of the soldiers would spend time with young ladies during the evening. It was their way of breaking the boredom of military life. After being asked early by a lady about companionship status, I replied to her that I did not prefer to participate in the activities of my fellow soldiers. She gave me a beautiful smile and departed. I spent the evening drinking and conversing with fellow soldiers. I missed home very much and longed for my loved ones and girlfriend.

The weeks passed, and I was developing into a stronger young man. Mentally, I had endured my time away from home respectfully and held myself militarily together. My training at Fort Sill was coming to an end. The next phase of my military life was about to occur. It was time for me to take another leave home from the military. I was ready to return home after my advanced infantry training. I was supposed to be sent to the country of Germany, but because of an altercation with another soldier, my orders were changed to Vietnam. The altercation with the other soldier consisted of a fist fight.

I was taking a shower in the shower barracks near my sleeping barracks. There were several people taking showers, and I was the only Black person. As I washed and scrubbed, a white soldier made a remark toward my color. One of the white soldiers said, "Man, this shower sure feels great tonight." At that moment, another white soldier responded by saying, "Yes, it sure does, but it would be better if that nigger was not in here." I was overwhelmed by the remark, became furious, and approached the white soldier. I was in the shower barracks with no other Black soldiers and was ready to fight several white soldiers because of the derogatory statement made toward me. The sleeping barracks were close to the shower barracks, and my fellow Black soldiers overheard the yelling and came storming into the shower barracks. I had struck the soldier with my fist, and the others marched toward me.

One of the Black soldiers yelled out, "Is there a problem?"

I quickly gathered my clothes and exited the shower barracks. The next morning, I was ordered to report to the captain's office. I was told by the captain that I faced military charges for striking a fellow soldier. The charges were lowered from a court martial to a mere conduct charge because of the derogatory racial statement. The captain told me that my orders for Germany were being changed to Vietnam. Striking a fellow soldier was a serious offense, but the derogatory racial statement made by the soldier toward me was just as mentally and physically damaging. I was the only surviving son in my immediate family and did not have to serve in the military. I was looking forward to going to the country of Germany and enjoying the people and their country as well. Instead, my orders were changed to Vietnam, and I was not court-martialed by the army.

I accepted the decision of the post commander and prepared myself to make the trip to Vietnam. It was an exceedingly difficult decision to make for a young man of eighteen years of age. I truly had grown up and matured during the first two phases of my military training. There were several things that occurred in my life during my military training. My leaving home and being on my own and making decisions without my parents were among some of the major life-changing events for me.

We all must get older and face our own predicaments and responsibilities. It is the way of the world and part of being an adult.

I was happy that the first two phases of my military training were ending. The time had come once again to go back home and regroup. It was time to see the family and enjoy friends again. The time spent training in the army made me more thankful for my family and friends. There was a lot of pressure placed upon me mentally and physically, but it made me a better and stronger person.

CHAPTER 5

The Call to War

In the year 1966, I finished my basic training and my advanced infantry training. I was once coming home for military leave. It was summer and an enjoyable time for getting around in Los Angeles, California. This would be the last leave that I received from the military before going to Vietnam. I was glad to return home and talk and share moments of joy with my parents and sisters.

I visited my girlfriend at her house after resting at home. I noticed that she seemed to react differently toward me than before I left. It seemed that the feelings that we shared prior to my leaving were not the same. Things can change during periods of time. I talked with her for several hours and enjoyed the conversation, but realized that our relationship was different from before. I spent much of my leave visiting relatives and friends and enjoying the atmosphere of Los Angeles, California. The days seem to past quickly, and I thought about the day of my return to the military base for overseas duty.

I was standing in the living room at the front window and felt a hand touch me on my shoulder. It was my father with a very serious look on his face. My father spoke in an incredibly soft tone about the change in my military orders and the problem with the army. He said he supported me 100 percent if I decided not to go back to the military base. I turned to my dad and gave him a hug with tears in my eyes. It was my dad's way of saying, "Do not go back." It was because of the prejudice event and the decision by the military to change my orders that he felt that way.

I took into consideration what my father had told me and turned to look out the front window again. I thought of all I had been through and came to a decision. I had always been a person who chose to complete things. Even as a gymnast in high school, I always made sure I gave my best to complete the challenge at hand. There were times in my younger life when I failed to complete certain things. I had dropped out of college prior to joining the army and quit various jobs. This time, I decided to continue my quest and let my God in heaven be the judge.

I told my father I would go back to the army and complete my tour of duty. I realized the dangers of the Vietnam tour of duty and what could occur. It was another major decision on my behalf concerning my responsibilities. I felt that I had made the correct decision and was ready to face my future militarily.

The day came closer to my return to the base for overseas duty. It was midsummer in the year 1966. I had finished my second leave at home and prepared for embarkment to the country of Vietnam. I was taken to a military airfield at Fort Ord, California. There were thousands of soldiers wanting to be taken to Vietnam. It was truly a remarkable sight of aircraft and military might. The lines moved extremely quickly and with complete precision. Soon, it was my turn to board my aircraft. As I boarded, I thought of my loved ones at home and what lies ahead for me.

CHAPTER 6

The War Zone

The trip to Vietnam seemed to take forever. The airplane flew endlessly. The first stop was in the state of Hawaii. We spent several hours there. I had never witnessed such beauty of green plant growth in one place before. The people were charming and the food was quite delicious. It was a state in the North American hemisphere, but seemed like another country. We soon had to reboard another aircraft for Vietnam once again. After boarding, I noticed that there were a group of special forces units on board. The soldiers of the special forces' sang and drank heavily as the aircraft made its way forward toward the country of Vietnam. The rest of the soldiers on board joined in their joyous festivities. The soldiers of the special forces unit decreased the level of fear and combat worry with their joyful attitudes.

During the flight, I looked out the window and saw a tiny mass of land. I asked one of the special forces about the land mass. He said it was the country called Guam. From the sky, it was not bigger than a pinhead, but very vital strategically for our missile systems. We were getting closer to the war zone of Vietnam. The anticipation of war would soon be a reality and fact. I closed my eyes and prayed to God for overall protection.

We had been traveling many hours by aircraft and were ready for the aircraft to land. Several hours after I woke from a good nap, the airplane pilot made an announcement over the airplane's intercom. He stated that we were entering the airspace of the country of Vietnam. At that moment, my heart seemed to beat at a faster pace. The anticipation of the trip to the war zone of Vietnam had finally ended. It was a noticeably brief time that the airplane landed. When the airplane landed, we were ordered to disembark the aircraft. The commanding officer gave the order to get all belongings off the airplane.

As I exited the military aircraft with my fellow soldiers, I saw hundreds and hundreds of other soldiers on the airstrip. The noise sounded like bees around their beehives. The movement of troops and military equipment seemed to go on continuously. It was truly a remarkable sight. The different commanding officers yelled out different orders to their troops. My commanding officer ordered us to get into formation. He told us what we were expected to do for the day and where to report for an assignment.

We were assigned to various military divisions and issued M16 automatic weapons. I was assigned to a division called The Big Red One. The Big Red One was an artillery support unit for the army infantry and special forces units. The Big Red One had earned its colors during combat campaigns during World War II. Earning colors simply meant the display of honor and bravery. The reality of combat was now at hand.

During my childhood, I watched war movies on TV, but now, it was a reality. Different thoughts ran through my mind about different things. The training we had received during our phases of military training was now ready to be utilized. I was assigned temporary sleeping barracks and given sleeping gear. I was exhausted from the picking up of uniform supplies and military commands. The assigned sleeping area was not like home, but felt good enough to lie down and get some well-deserved rest.

As I lay quietly sleeping, I was awakened by a loud noise and soldiers yelling in the barracks. Yells of getting down and taking cover went through the entire barracks. I quickly jumped from my bed and landed on the floor. The loud noise was a gunshot coming from the outer perimeter of the military base. This was my first encounter with the enemy and my first time under enemy gunfire. The enemy was the feared Viet Cong of North Vietnam. The Viet Congs came from the north of Vietnam and were controlled by communists. They wanted to take control of the southern portion of Vietnam and make it a communist sector also. This was what the entire Vietnam War was about.

After several days in the holding area for the new arrivals, I was assigned to my military post in the Republic of Vietnam. The post was near the city of Saigon, South Vietnam. It was in a very dense jungle area of the country. Several other soldiers and I were taken by helicopter to the artillery post. When we arrived, we were assigned to various artillery guns. The artillery guns consisted of various sizes. There were guns mounted on tanks and single artillery guns. We were drilled on several types of artillery guns. I was trained in my advanced artillery training, so I had no trouble operating the artillery guns.

The training on the artillery guns was very strenuous work, both physically and mentally. After operating the large guns, you would desire a delicious meal and rest. The climate of South Vietnam was quite different from the North American hemisphere. The temperature seemed to always be warm and extremely humid. It could be almost a hundred degrees and raining at the same time. It, indeed, was hard to get used to. The people of the country were quite pleasant in nature. I found the older Vietnamese and the younger delightful. The younger children made it a habit to try selling contraband to all soldiers. They sold things like cigarettes, whiskey, and marijuana. They were happy little people considering their dilemma. They lived in a war zone of total death and destruction, but managed to always have pleasant atmospheres with them. They utterly amazed me with their abilities to wake every day with smiles on their faces. The people themselves amazed me with their way of life and their humane feelings for life itself.

I often wondered how this war could exist with such loving people. I became good friends with some of the village locals and their families. The papa and mama son of a village often invited me to have dinner with them and the family. I felt at home and thought of my family back in America. They had given me the nickname Unhilo. I enjoyed the dinner of cooked chicken and mixed vegetables served by the mama son and her daughters. The daughters made me feel completely at home and served me with loving consideration. Their care for me reminded me of my family back home and their loving ways.

I had been in the country of Vietnam for almost two months and got used to its atmosphere. I arrived in the country in the month of September 1966. It was now approaching November 1966. My unit was getting ready to celebrate Thanksgiving. This was my first Thanksgiving away from home. I had not been in any combat and was worried about the time it would happen. I enjoyed Thanksgiving under the circumstances and feasted on the dinner that was served. The dinner was exceptionally good, and I did not ponder on the thought of combat.

After dinner, I returned to my barracks and finished writing some letters. The letters were to my parents and girlfriend. A few days later, there was talk of a major military operation coming up for our division. This would be the very first combat for me, and my fellow soldiers as well. It was standard procedure to give soldiers leave to the nearest noncombat city before a battle. The closest city was the city of Saigon, Vietnam.

The city of Saigon was equal to the hustle and bustle of a major city. People filled the streets, and the sound of car horns could be heard from every direction. There were hundreds of small bars that lined the main streets of Saigon. Beautiful girls stood in front of each bar and gave a look of sexual desire. We had been warned by our superior officers to take caution in sexual participation. There had been known cases where the enemies were Viet Cong hookers. These prostitutes had been known to insert various objects into their private parts to damage American soldiers physically. It was frightening to even think about and made one think twice about having sex.

The atmosphere in the bars was that of a busy night club. The girls were, indeed, beautiful and made one feel at home. All the women working in the bars in the city of Saigon were given mandatory venereal shots by the military. The city entertainment was particularly good and surprising. The Vietnamese singers were extremely good at imitating several types of music. They could imitate R&B, rock, and other sounds of music. It was good to be able to release some pressure from the war, but we were all careful of the surroundings we were in. We could not forget this was a war zone and to stay alert.

The time spent in the city of Saigon was worth the trip. My fellow soldiers and I seemed to be more relaxed and ready to continue with the military duties at hand. There was increased talk of a combat mission for my division. The mission was finally scheduled for the northern border of South Vietnam. My division was moved into combat to support special forces and army infantry. This was my first combat assignment, and I had a degree of fear. I prepared myself as well as I could with my military training and prayer.

As we drove the jungle roads, which were cut out by the army engineering corps, I could see the smoke from various bombs in the distance. The gunfire of helicopters and air force jets pounded the earth with bullets and bombs. My convoy continued to move forward down the empty road at a fast speed. We were nearing the special forces unit of the Eighty-Second Airborne. They were the best of the best army fighters.

In the area where they had been fighting, there were burned-out sections of the jungle. The fighting had been intense, and the smell of death was everywhere. From the top of the tank I was riding on, I saw many bodies lying on the burned-out jungle ground. They were the bodies of the special forces we had been sent to support. The Viet Cong had overrun their defenses and killed every soldier in the unit. It was a horrifying view and mentally devastating for a soldier of eighteen years of age. There was sorrow and anger at the same time among my fellow soldiers and myself.

To witness the actual loss of human life at the level seen was unbelievable. My unit moved on forward coming closer to the Viet Cong who had attacked and killed my fellow soldiers. As our artillery guns came closer to the enemy, my unit prepared for what we had been trained for. The Viet Cong was only several miles from the range of our artillery guns. Our artillery guns could fire projectiles of death at great distances and hit the target precisely.

The order was given to exit the tanks and prepare the artillery for gunfire. Never had I seen that many men move at the same time with such precision and speed toward combat. The artillery guns are angled and aligned by quadrants and deflections. These principles give the artillery guns their range of fire. We aimed our guns at the given orders and released total death to whatever they hit.

The firing continued for hours as the artillery guns delivered their deadly bombs. The smoke from the artillery guns covered the surrounding area. The order was given to stop firing the artillery guns. It had been a firing mission of support and one of revenge. We were notified by radio communications that all the Viet Cong were dead. Hundreds had paid the price for the slaughter of the Eighty-Second Airborne. The feeling of unity was one of satisfaction and overall completion of duties. The enemy had been defeated, and my unit had not taken any heavy losses. Our commanding officer congratulated the entire unit on its performance. We were given the order to pack up our gear and head back to our home base camp.

This had indeed been a wonderful experience for me, mentally and physically. As I rode on the M109 Howitzer gun, different things crossed my mind. I had survived my first major combat battle, and I was grateful. I thought of the times of peace and tranquility at home. Now things were different, and I had to act accordingly. I had to constantly be alert and on my guard for my safety.

It was not easy to go day by day with the same alert level. Eventually, a soldier learned to make this a regular practice if he or she wanted to survive in a war zone. I did not ask to come to Vietnam and fight in a devastating war. The hands of fate had ordered my path, and I had to adjust myself to the situation at hand. I now had to fulfill my duty as an American soldier and complete my duty and call to war. In this first battle, I fought as an American soldier; it taught me the true meaning of the word *patriotism*.

No one wants to fight in a war, but one must protect himself and others who protect one another. There is a very thin line between right and wrong. Through the ages, men have gone to war over different things. Once involved in such things as war, one must complete their task as a soldier. If the tour of duty is not complete, the consequences can be disastrous.

CHAPTER 7

The Battle of the Iron Triangle

The weeks and months passed, and the military duties of combat continued. I arrived in the country of Vietnam in September 1966, and now it was December 1967. Many things occurred while in the country of Vietnam. Some things had changed back home regarding my personal life with my girlfriend.

I was reading one of her letters in our home base barracks. She informed me that she had met someone else and seriously dating him. I felt extremely letdown about her changing her mind about our relationship. I thought of the times we told our feelings for each other. We must be able to accept whatever comes our way. I had to mentally adjust my emotions and accept the fact that she had chosen another in my place. It was not easy to respect her decision, but it was the right thing to do. This happened to other soldiers in my unit, and I had to comfort them. Now it happened to me, and other soldiers chose to comfort me. It was that way in the war zone of Vietnam.

My fellow soldiers and I fought side by side and shared one another's disappointments. It did not matter what nationality you were; we felt one another's traumas. That is one thing about war; people must care for one another even more so for survival. The laws of Jim Crow did not and could not exist in the battle zone of Vietnam. It is truly a shame that people must undergo such trauma to acquire such respect for each other.

I met and became good friends with a Caucasian soldier named John. John came from the Midwest, and we shared many interests as soldiers. We would both comfort each other in moments of sorrow and joy. I had many Black soldiers as friends, but John was equal to them in friendship. It was a unique experience to have a close friend so caring.

My unit had been assigned several other orders for combat after our first battle. We had completed all the assignments with bravery and honor. I had seen several of my fellow soldiers wounded and killed in combat. The artillery guns were in less danger than the infantry as far as accumulating casualties. The Viet Cong fought us on a continuous basis, using anything and everything that could lame or kill American soldiers. A soldier had to be extremely careful if he or she left their post. There were booby traps placed all around the perimeter of the main base camp. We were not allowed to go off base after hours, but some soldiers did.

I made the mistake of leaving the base one night without permission, and it was an extremely dangerous thing to do. I got bored and wanted to visit the Vietnamese family I knew. The daughters of the mama son really liked me, and I liked them. I exited our military base and climbed over the security fence. It was a route soldiers took to get to the local village. I made my way to the village and to the dwellings of my Vietnamese family. They were glad to see me and welcomed me to their house. The beautiful sisters served me beverages and wine. The papa son told me that Viet Congs were in the area, and it was not safe for me to stay.

As I talked and socialized with the family, a small child came running through the front door of the hut. The child was screaming, "VC! VC!" which meant that Viet Congs were entering the village, and I was in danger. If I was taken by the Viet Cong, I could have been killed or made a prisoner of war. I was quickly taken to a hiding place for my safety. If I were taken prisoner or killed in the village, it would mean military retaliation from America forces.

I quietly lay still while the Viet Cong walked through the village. Some of them entered the place where I was hiding. Never in my life did I feel the fear that I felt at that moment. The fear I felt was much greater than in my first combat battle. I held my breath until the Viet Cong made their exit from the hut and village. After the Viet Cong left, the mama son told me to come out of hiding. I quickly made my way back to the place where I had come. I would later find out that it was not the same place of entry. I had entered the opposite side of the base, and the ground was not level. There were holes in the ground from previous tank emplacements. The holes were at least three feet deep and difficult to walk across.

As I made my way across the mud-filled field, it was a complete challenge to reach my military barracks. After tracking through the muddy field, I finally reached the other security fence and climbed into safety. My fellow soldiers saw the mud on me and asked what happened. I told them what happened, and they broke out in laughter. After that incident, I never made another trip to the village after dark.

The combat battles continued to go on, and my unit continued to answer our call of duty. Little did I know that a battle of all battles was about to take place. It would be a life-changing event for me. The year was 1967, and the war in Vietnam continued to rage on. My unit was called up to support special forces and infantry in the Mekong Delta. The Mekong Delta was a strip of land mass located along the Cambodian border. It was extremely close to the Republic of North Vietnam.

The Viet Cong of the north was trying to move thousands of troops across the South Vietnam border. It made for a true battle to come between the two opposing armies. The American and South Vietnamese forces had to not allow the North Viet Cong to enter with such a great army. A fight to the death was at hand. We made the trip to the Mekong Delta and awaited the Viet Cong's arrival. The enemy was spotted approaching the South Vietnam border. My unit was given the orders to open fire on the oncoming enemy.

At the orders of our commander, we opened fire on the oncoming enemy. The cannon fire was consistent, and the guns fired nonstop until they begin to smoke. One of the artillery guns next to my gun crew exploded, and the gun crew was burned to a cinder. It was horrifying to look upon. Some of the soldiers had been killed, and others walked around like zombies. The rest of the artillery gun crews looked in shock. The artillery had fired so much that a round exploded in the chamber of the gun barrel.

At that moment, several of the gun crews refused to continue firing their artillery pieces. My gun crew was one of the ones that refused to commence firing. We were afraid of the artillery gun overheating, so we refused the order. The commanding officer informed us that we would receive disciplinary action for not following orders. After the guns cooled off, by pouring water on the barrels, we once again commenced fire on the orders given. We still faced the summary court martial.

The enemy of the North was defeated, and the South Vietnamese army and American army were victorious. The Battle of the Iron Triangle was over, but retaliation for not following orders awaited several soldiers. I was one of the soldiers awaiting disciplinary from commanding officers. I was confronted by the commanding officer of our base to report to a military hearing. After the hearing, several of my gun crew members and I were sent back to our barracks to await the decision of the military court. It was not long before our first sergeant informed us of the decision of the military court. We had been found guilty of not following a direct order. Several of my gun crew members and I were sentenced to ninety days in a military jail. It was a very depressing feeling, and we all felt incredibly sad.

This would go on our military records and delay our chances for rank promotions. Later, we were relocated on military trucks and taken to the military jail in the city of Long Binh Vietnam. The trip itself took several hours, going through safe areas of travel. The city of Long Binh Vietnam had been conquered by American forces and was a secure area. After arriving at the jail, we were assigned to various barracks and given jail identification cards. This was something entirely different for me.

Looking at the jail compound and the barbwire around the jail walls was extremely humiliating. I truly felt sorrow for disobeying the direct order when in combat. There were hundreds of soldiers walking around the stockade. The stockade was run on the same principle as the military units in the combat areas of Vietnam. All inmates were awakened in the early dawn hours and given breakfast and assigned various duties in the stockade and within the city of Long Binh itself. The duties in the stockade consisted of maintaining the prison grounds and working in the stockade kitchen. The duties within the city of Long Binh consisted of building and refortifying bunkers. The duty consisted of feeling sandbags and digging deep trenches. These bunkers were scattered throughout the city of Long Binh for the protection of civilian and military personnel.

The work was extremely hard and demanded a lot from each soldier physically. The days passed in the stockade, and I had completed several weeks of my sentence. One morning, a stockade guard ordered everyone to wake up and report for their usual assignments. That morning, I was extremely tired from the previous day and refused to get out of bed. The guard ordered me to get up a second time, but I still refused to rise from my bed. After the second order from the guard, I was woken up by several stockade guards and taken out of the barracks. I was then taken to the stockade headquarters and given punishment for my failure to follow an order.

I was given thirty days in solitary confinement. I was then taken to the solitary confinement section and placed into a small cell. The cell was about six feet long and four feet long. The stockade officials called the small cell a box. There were no windows on the walls and no restrooms either. Inmates were let out to use the restrooms upon request and then returned to their cells. In order to go to the restroom, a soldier had to yell out to the guard each time. It was very degrading. The only form of entertainment I was allowed to participate in was the reading of the Bible.

I read my Bible daily and was comforted in many ways. I began to let go of some of the hostile feelings about the war. I began to understand the feelings of the military court and owned my conviction. I was wrong in the eyes of the military and accepted my sentence of jail time. I was sentenced to thirty days in the hole, and the days were ending.

As I spent my time in the small cell reading my Bible and singing, I could not wait for the time and punishment to be over. I had been keeping track of the days of confinement in the small cell. I was in the small cell sleeping when I heard a voice through the small window at the door of the cell. It was one of the guards with orders for my release and return to the outer stockade grounds. This was truly a happy moment for me. It had been thirty days for me without any other human contact. I had been placed on a diet of bread and water for several days of my solitary confinement.

After getting back to the main population of the stockade, I was returned to my barracks once more. I was released in time enough for the dinner meal in the stockade. It had been some time since I had a decent meal. I was glad to look upon regular food once again. The next time I was told to rise for the morning stockade formation, I quickly did so.

The days continued to pass in the stockade, and my sentence was ending. Prior to my release day from the stockade, I was taken with a group of fellow inmates and addressed by the commander of the Long Binh stockade. The commander stated we had served our time and had two choices to make concerning our military futures. He stated the first choice was to go back to the war zone of Vietnam or observe prison time in the United States of America. The prison time would be served at Leavenworth Penitentiary. I quickly processed what the military official had said and promptly made my decision. If I chose to go to prison and be back in America, I would be dishonorably discharged, and my life would be in complete disorder. I would have my freedom from the combat zone but still serve prison time in America. I joined the United States Army, and completing my tour of duty was especially important to me. I realized what a dishonorable discharge would mean. The thought of spending any amount of prison time in Leavenworth Prison was unacceptable.

I told the commanding officer to return me to active duty and back to the artillery unit. The following day, I was loaded into an army truck and returned to my artillery command center. I was back in the war zone again and ready to complete my tour of duty. The mistakes were behind me, and ahead of me lay my military future. I wanted to come back home with honors, not with disgrace.

CHAPTER 8

A Short Time Left in the Country

Upon my return to my base camp headquarters, I was truly welcomed back by my fellow soldiers. It had been three months, and it was good to see the soldiers I had been through so much with. The combat firing missions continued, and the days turned into months. The ninety days spent in the stockade made my time in the war zone longer by three months. The time spent in the stockade did not count toward the tour of duty time spent in Vietnam. The months passed by and turned into a shorter time in the combat zone for me.

It was the year 1967, and the Viet Congs were still giving strong amounts of resistance. One evening while everyone was simply resting and enjoying themselves, all hell broke loose with incoming rocket fire and enemy gunfire. The Viet Congs were attacking our base camp; all gun crews were ordered to report to their artillery guns in defense of our base camp. The Viet Cong penetrated our perimeter, which could mean death to all. The battle to preserve our lives and the security of the base camp was on. The enemy was all around the base camp, and the fighting was fierce.

The artillery guns fired directly into the surrounding jungle of the base camp. There were helicopters in the air firing continuous rounds of automatic machine gunfire. They fired into the surrounding jungle, killing everything in sight. The artillery guns blasted all sides of the perimeter of the base camp. Every soldier moved at a rapid pace, loading and firing their artillery guns. I was busy loading my artillery gun with dozens of types of powder charges.

As I was throwing an empty canister into a pile of empty ones, something hit my right hand, and pain shot through my right arm. Someone had thrown an empty canister and hit my right hand, taking off the tip of my right finger. I yelled out in pain as other gun crew members came to my aid. My first sergeant yelled out, "Get the tip of his finger off the ground." The tip of my right ring finger was picked up, and I was taken to the hospital. I was shipped by helicopter to the main hospital in the city of Long Binh located in Vietnam. It was another time of trauma for me, and I was worried about my condition.

At the hospital, I was prepped for my surgery. The attending physician reattached the tip of my finger to my right hand. There was a possibility that the nerves would grow together, and the amputated piece of finger would not be infected. Days passed and the tip of my finger was still connected to my hand. My attending doctor examined it daily to look for infection. After several days, my doctor told me of the status of the reattached finger. He stated that there was a chance that a condition called gangrene could possibly set in. The condition was an infection that could spread from one part of the body to another. This could cause deterioration of other parts of the body and keep spreading.

He stated I had to make a major decision about the tip of my finger. I could leave the tip of my finger on and risk more infection or have it removed for my own safety. It was an extremely hard decision to make. I didn't want to lose the tip of my finger, but I made up my mind to remove the tip of my finger. I did not want to risk getting any more of the gangrene infection in my hand. If it spread, I could lose my entire life.

I rehabbed in the military hospital for several weeks. I was depressed about the loss of the tip of my right ring finger, but relieved about the gangrene infection not spreading throughout my entire body. I spent a month getting better in the hospital for the condition of my finger. My doctor informed me of my upcoming release from the military hospital and return to active duty. I returned to my base camp for active duty. Due to the injury of my right hand, I was placed on light duty. I no longer had to work on the artillery guns and do any extreme lifting. I was assigned to work in the mess hall and kitchen and other lighter assignments. My time remaining in the Vietnam War zone was finally ending. The days had accumulated, and I had become a short-timer.

The term *short-timer* was given to those soldiers who had limited time left in the war zone. It was a time that a lot of soldiers worried about their safety even more than usual. I had seen other soldiers for short periods of time, killed before they went home. One was my first sergeant of our gun crew. He had only days left in the war zone and was killed. He was killed while trying to protect an ammunition dump from being blown up by the Viet Cong. Viet Congs were spotted around the ammo dump of our base camp, placing explosive charges. Our first sergeant charged toward the ammo dump and confronted the enemy. He killed several of the Viet Cong before he himself was killed by enemy gun fire. It was a terrible thing to witness by each soldier. Things like that happened very often in the war zone of Vietnam. Therefore, soldiers took extra precautions when there was a brief time left in the country.

The loss of our first sergeant was a great loss to my gun crew and myself. The first sergeant was like a father image to us, and we missed him very much. My time got shorter in the country as the Vietnamese Tet Holiday approached. The Vietnamese Tet Holiday celebrates the arrival of spring in the country of Vietnam. The North Vietnamese decided to push forward with a full attack on all American and South Vietnamese military forces.

It was now 1968, and my time left in Vietnam was only a few weeks. I was worried about the Viet Cong attacking before I got my orders to depart Vietnam. With only days left in the country of Vietnam, the Viet Cong launched a full assault on American and South Vietnamese military forces. This battle was called the Tet Offensive and was one of the bloodiest battles between American and South Vietnamese forces. It would cost the lives of thousands of American and South Vietnamese forces.

I was in my barracks when rocket and mortar explosions pounded our base camp. There were so many incoming projectiles, and it was difficult to know where they came from. My fellow soldiers and I ran out of our barracks to seek protection. I was hit by a piece of shrapnel in my upper lip, and it went down my throat. Later, I found out that the piece of metal had damaged me internally.

I ran out of the barracks with my M16 automatic machine gun. I was trying to reach the safety of the bomb shelter several yards away. I ran for a while before a rocket landed close to me. The blast of the rocket blew me off the ground into the air. I sailed through the air for some time before hitting the ground. After landing on the ground, I noticed my location. I had landed on the top of sands bags in front of the bunker. I called out in pain for help. I had been wounded very badly.

Others who had made it to the bunker before me gave me assistance. I was given morphine for the pain and other medical attention. I was wounded badly, but had to wait for the bombs to stop falling. It seemed like the bombardment of our base would never end. Finally, the incoming projectiles stopped falling. I was then placed into a military ambulance by nurses and taken to the field hospital.

These field hospitals were comparable to regular hospitals but located directly within a combat zone itself. If not for these field hospitals, thousands of soldiers would have died from combat wounds. My Caucasian friend, John, had chosen to ride with me in the ambulance. He was a good friend, indeed, putting his own life in jeopardy. While the military ambulance rushed me to the field hospital, bombs were falling close to the vehicle.

At the field hospital, I was placed on an operating table. My wounds were extreme, and I would have to be taken out of the field hospital. I was placed by attendants and put aboard a medical helicopter, then rushed to the main hospital in the city of Long Binh, Vietnam. When I arrived at the main hospital in Long Binh, Vietnam, I was placed in a holding area. I was awakened by the sound of voices and saw various people walking around. They were doctors and nurses who attended to the combat wounded.

One of the attending nurses checked my pulse and ordered me to surgery. As I looked around, I could see many other soldiers with white sheets over their heads. I felt blessed that I was still alive and that the Lord kept me alive. I woke up the following day after my surgery on the hospital ward floor. I had been through a great ordeal, mentally and physically. A military doctor assigned to me examined me fully. He told me of the seriousness of my wounds and how fortunate I was to be alive.

The wounds that I had sustained were deadly, but amazingly, I survived. I went through a phase of depression because of my injuries. I lay next to another soldier and asked him how he was doing. He was a South Vietnamese with serious wounds. The soldier smiled at me and said he was getting along. A nurse came to bathe him and tend to his wounds.

As she pulled back the covers on his bed, I saw injuries he had sustained to his lower body. The soldier had lost the entire portion of his body from his stomach down to his feet. After seeing such courage displayed by the wounded soldier, my depression and attitude changed for the better. I had to learn to walk and control my body all over again. I would often not want to get up and exercise, but the attending nurse made me do so. She told me if I did not, I would become paralyzed and never walk again. That made me get up very quickly.

Several days had passed during my stay in the hospital. A nurse approached me one morning with my medications and breakfast. I was told that a high-ranking colonel was to visit the hospital ward. Later, I was approached by the officer at my bedside. The officer had paperwork in his hand and a small purple box. He spoke to me about my wounds and how blessed I was to survive them. He then presented me with paperwork and the medal of the Purple Heart.

The Purple Heart medal was only presented to soldiers who had been wounded in combat. It was one of our nation's highest military medals given for wounds received in combat. I felt proud to receive my Purple Heart. The colonel said that he wanted to pin the medal on me personally, but he did not know where to put it because of the many combat wounds on my body. He, the entire medical staff, and I broke out in joyful laughter.

I spent several weeks in the hospital in the city of Long Binh, Vietnam. My attending physician decided I could be taken and transported out of Vietnam to the country of Japan. There, I would finish my recuperations from my war wounds. I was incredibly happy to hear the news; it meant I was on my way back to America and home. It had been a long time coming, and I was truly thankful to God for my survival.

In a few days, I was placed on a medical military aircraft and transported to the country of Japan. My tour of duty ended in the year 1968. It ended with me being wounded and transported to another country. Still, I was glad to be on my way back to the United States of America.

CHAPTER 9

Back to the World

Soldiers with short periods of tour duty would often shout out the slogan, "Back to the world!" The slogan meant a soldier was going home to the American shores. His duty in the war zone was over, and he had survived the war zone. It was a slogan that all American soldiers longed to shout out.

Before boarding the medical aircraft for the country of Japan, I could not help from yelling the traditional slogan; it was a moment of complete joy and mental satisfaction. I was now on my way to the country of Japan to complete my recovery from my combat wounds. The aircraft was filled with many wounded soldiers.

It was hard for me to breathe at times because of my lung injuries. The injuries were sustained from pieces of shrapnel. Shrapnel was tiny pieces of metal that came from enemy projectiles. Some of those particles had entered my body after a bomb exploded next to me.

The aircraft flew continuously toward the country of Japan with its cargo of wounded American soldiers. The medical aircraft finally landed on the airstrip in Japan. I was then placed aboard a military ambulance and taken to the main hospital in the city of Osako, Japan. The hospital was extremely huge in size and could hold thousands of combat-wounded soldiers. I was taken to the hospital and attended by various nurses and doctors.

My wounds were examined and I was assigned to a hospital ward. The nurses were very attentive in every way. Several days had passed and I wanted to make a call home. The hospital there had access to phone service. It had been a long time since I had spoken to my family by phone. I had gotten well enough to speak with a regular voice tune and hold a lengthy conversation. It had taken a long time for me to get strong enough to reach this level.

As I picked up the telephone, I thought of the things I had been through. For weeks, I could not speak and was too weak physically to even get out of my bed. Now, I was about to call home and speak with my parents. This was a moment I had dreamed. I dialed my parents' phone number and it rang several times. Finally, the phone stopped ringing and my mother picked up the phone. I said hello to her and asked how she was doing. She could not hold back the tears and started crying frantically. I could not hold back the tears either.

We both spent several moments crying. She asked me if it was really me on the phone and where was I located. I consoled her and told her it was me, and I was in the country of Japan. My mother continued to talk to me with tears in her voice. I was so glad to hear my mother's voice. My father got on the phone and asked the same question as my mother did. I told my dad that I was recuperating in the Japan hospital and would be coming home shortly.

The United States Army had sent a letter to my parents about my wounds. The letter said that I was critically wounded. My parents were worried about if was killed in action or not. Both were overjoyed to hear my voice; it assured them I was all right. I spoke with my parents for several minutes before a nurse came to my bedside. She told me that I had spoken long enough on the phone and not to exhaust myself physically. I told my parents what the nurse had said. My parents said goodbye to me with a joyous tone of voice. I genuinely enjoyed the conversation with my parents. I was a bit physically exhausted from the conversation, but mentally joyous in every way.

The nurse then gave me my evening medication. The pain in my wounds seemed lighter after the conversation with my parents. Later, I would find out why my mother cried during our conversation. It was because she had a premonition of me being wounded. She told me that she saw me crawling through the hallway of our house covered with blood. It is utterly amazing when people can see such events before they occur. My mother was a deeply religious type of person and so was my father. I do believe that their faith and prayers for me played a major part in my survival of the Vietnam War.

My days in the hospital in Japan were peaceful, and I was getting stronger and stronger as time went by. My combat wounds were healing at a fantastic pace, and I was beginning to walk around the hospital ward. I had been in the Japan hospital for several weeks and began to get my appetite back more and exercising more. I was walking more, eating more, and starting to feel like my old self. The combat wounds still gave me certain levels of pain, but exercising helped in many ways.

Several weeks passed, and I had been talking to my loved ones at home and got used to getting out of bed and bathing on my own. I was truly getting back to my regular routines. My attending physician told me I was strong enough to take a trip to the inner city. I told the doctor I would like to take a trip to the city with other soldiers. This was my first time out of a medical facility in months, and I welcomed the opportunity to travel.

I was loaded into a van with other veterans and taken to the inner city of Osaka, Japan. The city reminded me of the busy streets of Los Angeles, California. There were thousands of cars on the streets and people walking and running everywhere. It was an exceptionally large metropolitan city. As we toured the city, we stopped at various places of business. The restaurants were full of people and the stores were as well. We shopped and brought things that we liked for ourselves and for our nurses. We had a particularly enjoyable time in the city of Osaka, Japan.

The day was ending and it was time for us to return to the military hospital. It had been a beautiful trip, and all the disabled were ready to get back to the barracks. There were Japanese gangs that filled the streets of the city at night. It was not safe for American soldiers to be on the streets of Japan after dark.

The people in the city of Osaka were genuinely nice in nature. Everywhere we went, the people treated us with respect and honor.

I found the stories to be true about Japanese culture. They are truly well-cultured people and very hospitable to other cultures. It was time for me to be sent back to the shores of the United States of America. I became physically and mentally stronger, but I still required medical attention. I was taken to the airstrip in Osaka, Japan, for my flight to America.

* ⭐ *

CHAPTER 10

The Homecoming

I faced many different tests and trials during my travels in the military. I was only eighteen years of age when I entered the armed forces. I was now twenty-one years of age and had witnessed many dramatic events. There were events of joy and sorrow. Some things that occurred to me were those of godly spiritual nature. My survival of the war wounds and injuries I got while in Vietnam was among the most spiritual of all. Some of the other things that occurred were traumatizing things during the Vietnam combat. It was something an individual could not and would not forget for the rest of their living days.

Surviving any war under combat conditions was more than just human endurance. After witnessing events in the war zone in Vietnam, I must assuredly believe in the spiritual element of God. So much happened to me that could have been detrimental. Many doctors looked at me in awe and wondered how I survived my wounds. After their examinations, they would walk away in amazement and disbelief.

When the military aircraft landed in Fort Ord, California, I was overjoyed and ready to exit the aircraft. I exited the aircraft and was taken to the military hospital at Fort Ord, California. The trip by airplane had given me somewhat of a medical setback. The cabin air pressure was too heavy on my lungs, and I felt ill from the long and exhausting trip. I was immediately taken to the ward of the Fort

Ord hospital. The doctors examined me, and I was placed in a hospital ward once again. My parents were notified about my condition and told not to visit me. They were instructed to wait until I was stronger to receive visitors.

Several days passed, and I was becoming much stronger and allowed visitors. My parents came several weeks after my return to the Fort Ord hospital. They were glad to see me, and I was glad to see them. They both were talking with smiles on their faces and were very joyful. It had been such a long time since I had enjoyed my parents in person. Their visit lasted for several hours before they had to leave. I told them that I had only a brief time in the army and would be discharged in about two months. They were happy to hear that and left with cheerful goodbyes.

The year was 1968, and it was the month of April. It was springtime in the state of California. It had been several weeks since my parents had visited and I was getting much stronger. I was walking around the hospital ward and watching TV in the hospital lodge. One morning, I was lying in bed and I heard yelling in the hospital ward. I wondered what the noise could possibly be. I then heard people saying different things about Martin Luther King Jr. I overheard the shocking news that Martin Luther King Jr. had been assassinated. The shock was overwhelming and mentally devastating.

I constantly cried and felt extreme sadness about his death. Several days later, my attending military doctor informed me of my discharge from the Fort Ord hospital. I was discharged from the hospital and assigned to regular barracks. It reminded me of the first time I had come to Fort Ord as a trainee. Now I had been to war, wounded in combat, and returned home with military honors. It was not an easy task to complete, and it was a blessing to complete my military tour of duty. My time in the military was concluding. I had been written up as a wounded war veteran and given extremely light duty assignments around the base.

I spent most of my time resting and preparing for my discharge. Prior to my discharge, my commanding officer called me into the command office. The commanding officer talked to me about my plans after leaving the army. He asked me if I would like to reenlist and be assigned to the country of Germany. The idea of a trip to Germany and a promotion in rank was an exceptionally good offer. I had been through so much while in the army, and I felt I could not endure another tour of military duty.

I told the commander that I only wanted to go home. He looked at me with understanding and signed my discharge papers. He explained to me various things about my discharge papers. My discharge papers were both honorable and of a medical discharge. I accepted the papers and prepared myself to exit the military base of Fort Ord, California. My last days on base were spent returning military equipment and signing military documents. I had spoken to my parents about military discharge and my coming home. They were overjoyed and told me that my old room was ready and to hurry home.

The day arrived for me to exit the military base of Fort Ord, California. I was transported to the local Greyhound bus station in the city of Monterey Bay, California. It would be the last time I would ride in a military vehicle and take any more military orders. It was truly a feeling of freedom and I had to get used to the idea of a nonmilitary lifestyle.

As the bus rolled toward the city of Los Angeles, California, I had to go into a moment of prayer and meditation. I was so very thankful to have survived the Vietnam War and all the other things that happened to me while in the military. The scenery of the coastline of California looked so very peaceful after seeing the war zone of Vietnam.

I closed my eyes and went to sleep with peace of mind and a feeling of serenity. The days of constant fear of combat were over, and the war zone of Vietnam was far away. It was, indeed, a physical and mental burden placed on every soldier in the war zone of Vietnam. The burden of physically fighting the war and the mental worry of staying alive were ongoing. These things never leave an individual's mind. With such trauma, a person can be expected to have memories of such events. The military would later call this condition PTSD.

The hours passed on the bus, and I got even more anxious to get back to my old homestead. I was anticipating what my mother would make for dinner and what the rest of the family was doing. The bus driver announced that we were on the outer boundaries of the city of Los Angeles, California. My heart beat a little faster as we came closer to the inner city of Los Angeles. I was home at last, and the city of Los Angeles never looked so good.

The bus eventually arrived at the Greyhound bus terminal in the heart of downtown Los Angeles, California. I exited the bus and went to the nearest public telephone. I made a call to my parents' house, and my mother answered the phone. I told her of my arrival from Fort Ord by bus, and I was waiting at the bus station. She told me to wait there for a few hours until my father came home from his job.

During the time I was waiting, it was pleasing to simply watch the people walk around. It had been a long time since I looked at actual citizens of my hometown. The time passed fast before my father made his way through the crowd of the bus terminal. He yelled out when he saw me sitting on one of the benches in the terminal's waiting area. I yelled back, "Dad, over here!"

My father gave me a hug, which seemed to last for an exceptionally long time. As he held me in his arms, he told me how much he missed me and welcomed me back home. My mother and sisters were at home preparing things for my arrival. The city looked the same in the downtown area. It was very relaxing to ride along as my father drove his car heading home. He asked me about my trip home from the Fort Ord military base and the medals on my uniform. I told him the trip from Fort Ord was great, and the medals on my uniform were issued for good conduct.

We were getting closer to our homestead and I was very anxious to see the rest of the family. My dad drove into the driveway of our house and I felt contentment. My dad parked the car and I made my way to the rear door of our house. The door opened and my mother and my two sisters gave me hugs. I was extremely glad to see all of them. It had been so exceptionally long since all of us looked upon one another's faces. It was a true blessing to be with them again after all the different occurrences during my military tour of duty. The atmosphere of the house relaxed me in every way.

My mother prepared a magnificent dinner for my homecoming. There were several different dishes on the dinner table. Everything I desired and was used to eating was there. Things like baked honey ham, southern fried chicken, mashed potatoes and gravy, turnip greens, black-eyed peas, and various tasty pies. I had longed for this moment for so exceptionally long it was like a dream come true.

Before we began eating, my father blessed the food on the table. We all gave thanks to the Lord for my safe return home. As I feasted on the delicious dinner my mother had prepared, my entire family laughed and talked of my return home and how good it was to be back together. This was truly a blessed event for me; it was something I desired for a long time. From the time spent in the military, I learned many different things about life in general. I had a better understanding of people and how to deal with other people on various levels. I also had a better understanding of survival, mentally and physically, under any conditions. The years in the military were, indeed, rough, and the war in Vietnam was as well. The years gave me experience in mental strength, but at the same time, it gave me levels of anguish.

CHAPTER 11

Destiny's Call

There are many people who know the meaning of the word *destiny*; but also, there are many who think that it has truly little to do with an individual's life. Everything that we do, I believe, is truly intended to occur. In each life, events happen to occur on an individual basis. Things will happen to each one of us, and those things are simply destined to occur. Some might say that it happened by coincidence or by a person's actions.

It is like making a comparison of rich and poor. Some individuals rise from extremely poor to extraordinarily rich, while others might start at the same level and remain at a similar level. That to me is a good example of destiny and things being meant for each of us. Many of the historical occurrences throughout time have amazed many theologians. There are questions about how smaller armies could defeat an army five or more its size. Some people would sum it up as something fortunate to occur. The more reasonable and rational answer to me would be simple destiny.

Destiny is a word defined as the events that will necessarily happen to a particular person or thing in the future. Also, it is stated to mean the hidden power to believe to control what will happen in the future, or fate.

After Vietnam, the years passed, and many things in America changed, and so did I. The seventies had come to America, and along with it were new social practices. A new group of young Americans called the hippies had developed into a national cult. They believed in having more love within society than war and social destruction. It was a new way of thinking for the younger generations of Americans. They enjoyed smoking their marijuana and making love. They lived in open communes with no racial boundaries.

Usually before entering a commune, all possessions were given away or given to the hippie commune itself. The social moods of the hippies were, indeed, one of peace and social acceptance for all races. There were those within America who did not want to comply with the hippies' lifestyle. They were the bigoted groups in American society. They were groups like the Ku Klux Klan and other groups of racial hatred.

I had been home for several years and simply resting and recuperating from the Vietnam War still. My wounds were still healing, both physically and mentally. My family had been very understanding to me and supported my medical recovery fully. If it had not been for my family, I would not have fully survived the aftermath of the Vietnam War. The 1970s were also a time for the Black revolutionaries of North America. Groups like the Black Panthers had risen in defense of Black civil rights on a state and federal level. This caused a social and political war of disturbances throughout the nation.

I was invited by one of my childhood friends to join the Black Panthers in Los Angeles, California. I told my childhood friend that I no longer wanted to use guns and I wanted peace and quiet. He turned from my front door and walked away. Later, I heard he was killed in a hail of gunfire during a robbery of a federal bank. I felt incredibly sad about the loss of my childhood friend, but glad that I was not there with the group of Black Panthers during the bank robbery.

Once again, the thought of destiny crossed my mind. I had been through one war and survived it. I believe to this date that it was not meant for me to meet my demise in such a manner. I was still recovering from the war wounds and making my annual trips to the Department of Veterans Administration. I had been going there since my homecoming and receiving medical treatment for the war wounds received in the war zone of Vietnam.

The years were tough for me after returning home. I was read-justing mentally, physically, and socially. The years of the seventies had passed, and the eighties were on the way. I adapted to society to a great degree. I chose not to join the hippies of the seventies and not to join the Black Panther party either. I mostly kept to myself and concentrated on my health. I eventually got stronger enough to move into my own apartment on the west side of Los Angeles. With the money I saved from the military, I could afford a small apartment. I also enrolled in college and was getting grant money from the State of California for my schooling.

The school I was attending was called Trade Technical College, in Los Angeles, California. I also received money from the Veterans Administration for disability. The combined income of the two sources allowed me to pay bills and finance an automobile. I was on my own and attending school to better my educational level and career opportunities. I still would go to my parents' house often for my mother's good cooking. I always enjoyed those visits with them any time of the year.

Things were going good in school and I enjoyed the atmosphere of the college campus. I was serious about my studies and wanted to graduate with an associate of arts degree. I became a member of the school speech team. My speech team was dominant in various com-petitions with other colleges in the state of California college region. We later went on to place third in a national competition at the national junior college tournament held in the state of Oklahoma.

While attending my speech classes, my speech instructor allowed the class to be visited by a famous actor and renowned speaker on multimedia circuits. His name was Roscoe Lee Browne. It was truly a pleasure to be in his presence. My meeting with the renowned actor made me more interested in the field of acting. I began to inquire about the field of acting and finding out how to submit myself for movies and other things related.

The years at Trade Technical College passed and I graduated in 1982. It had taken me longer than the required two years, but I managed to acquire my associate of arts degree. After my graduation from junior college, I then enrolled at California State University in Los Angeles, California. I attended California State University from 1982 through 1985. I ran into financial trouble while attending classes at the California State campus. My assistance from the government and Veterans Administration was no more. My GI bill was exhausted, and I had to pay for the last year of my classes on my own.

It was a very disappointing time for me as a young Black student. I only had a year before my graduation, but I could not afford the expensive courses required. I was forced to drop out of California State University. With only fifty upper units to complete, I was forced to drop out of school. I had to really adjust to the change in my life. After dropping out of school, I worked temporary jobs whenever I could. I decided to sign up with a movie casting company for casting calls. If you fit the role, they would call you for the part in a movie.

The company was called Central Casting. The 1980s were a terribly busy time for movies, and I received many background roles in various movies. I enjoyed the different movie sets and meeting many of the movie stars I had seen as a younger man. I also was singing in a nightclub in the West Los Angeles area of California. I had a friend of mine who was involved in the world of entertainment. He was a disc jockey and knew several celebrities. I was introduced to people like the legendary Marvin Gaye, Martha Reeves, Smokey Robinson, and countless others. My close friend, Will Jay Hill arranged for me to meet Marvin Gaye in his studio in the city of Hollywood, California.

I had some songs I had written and was trying to get them out on the market. Marvin was busy with different things at the time. He explained to me that he could not help me with my personal arrangements at the present time. He then told me not to give up my desires as a musician and to continue my quest. He also made a statement about destiny. It was his belief that destiny plays a significant role in everyone's life. It was the same belief that I had come to hold after my experiences in the Vietnam War. If something was meant to be, then it would simply come to be.

Even though my songs were not accepted by him at that time, I felt a sense of complete understanding and held no aggressive feelings. These are the feelings that a person will receive when they have a rational understanding of why things occur and do not retaliate against their occurrence. Having a destiny tends to be a true reality for each one of us. We often wonder why different things happen to some people and not others. Could it be that all our lives are in accordance with preordained destiny? Things happened throughout the history of humankind, which were unbelievable in their timely occurrence. These things were unexplainable sometimes in reasoning, but still, they helped in the continuation of life itself. Even some scholars have made the statement, "It was meant to be." After observing such events and confirming such miraculous events, one can only conclude that destiny might coincide with all our lives.

The years of the 1980s were ending, and I was working as an assistant schoolteacher in Los Angeles School District. The pay was good, and I enjoyed collaborating with the elementary school level. I worked the job with the school district for several years, but desired a higher base salary. I was reading the "Wanted" column one day and gazed upon a job position as a cab driver. I had often thought of the cab driving position as a low-paying job. It amazed me to see the amount of money that could be made. I also became interested in driving limousines. The driving positions paid high wages and I was interested in acquiring more money.

I first filled out an application for a position as a limousine driver. The company was in the city of Brentwood, California. Brentwood is in the area above Hollywood, California. The office of the limousine company was in the hotel lobby of the Holiday Inn. The company had extremely beautiful limousines. I was totally impressed with the cars and the hotel in general. I was hired by the company owner and became a limo driver.

I worked for a company called True Comfort for several years during the late 1980s. I made a particularly good salary while working at the company. The Holiday Inn hotel was in an extraordinarily rich area of the city. Its clients were usually movie stars and very wealthy. I had the opportunity to meet many movie and television celebrities. The job was, indeed, interesting. Not only did I meet celebrities at the cinema, but I also, at times, had to drive for gangsters.

I was assigned to pick up gangsters from Los Angeles, California, on one occasion. The owner told me that I did not have to accept the trip. The group from the city of Compton were members of the deadly gang the Crips. The limousine had been ordered for nine hours, which meant an exceptionally large payday. I accepted the trip and drove to pick up the clients. There were six of them, and they were all very well-dressed with gold and several types of expensive pieces of jewelry on them. They told me to take them to the city of Oxnard, California. I headed the limousine toward its destination. After driving for about half an hour, I was told by one of the gang members to pull over to a restaurant. They had become hungry and wanted to get something to eat. I did so, and the group began to exit the limousine. A member of the group asked me if I would like to join them for dinner. It was in a high-end restaurant and I accepted the invitation. The food was exceptionally good and I enjoyed it very much, but I also thought of the people I was eating with. I accepted the invitation because I did not want to be rude to a company client.

After dinner, everyone reentered the limousine and we were off to the city of Oxnard, California. The trip was eight hours round trip. As I drove the limo toward the city of Oxnard, I overheard the group speaking in the rear of the limo. They were talking very loudly; I could not help but hear them speaking. They were talking about killing one of their fellow gang members.

As they talked, I listened to all they had to say and then the whole conversation stopped. The front and rear sections of all limousines have a divider that separates the driver from the passengers. This is for the privacy of the passengers as well as the limo driver. I was asked by one of the gang members if I heard any of the things they had spoken. I quickly said, "No, I did not hear any of your private and personal conversations, and I was concentrating on my driving." We finally reached the city of Oxnard, and I was told to take them to one of the malls in the city to shop.

It was Christmas time and they came to the city to shop. I waited in the car for them to return from their shopping spree. When they were done shopping, they had many boxes and gifts for the holiday. They reentered the limo, and we headed back to the city of Los Angeles.

Driving back to Los Angeles, I thought of their conversations prior to our return to Los Angeles. I do believe that the quick response of not overhearing their conversation about killing someone truly saved my life.

The months passed, and the limo company was not doing as much business as usual. I had many experiences both good and bad with the limo company. I gained a lot of experience dealing with people and the traffic of the busy city of Los Angeles, California. I began to think about a position that offered more hours and pay for me in general. I thought about the cab driver position I had considered before I became a limo driver. I looked through the "Wanted" ads of the local newspaper to see what I could find. I came across a cab company called the Inglewood Cab Company. I went in for an interview and was hired by the cab company after a background check.

I had driven limousines, but had never driven a cab before. It was remarkably like the limo company, but the size of the vehicles was different. I would soon find out what the driving of cabs was all about. I was now a cab driver in the city of Inglewood, California, and I enjoyed the job. I worked five days a week and sometimes more. The pay that I made as a cab driver was higher compared to that of being a limo driver. I made, on average, two to three hundred dollars a day. The money was, indeed, good and gave me an incentive to continue with the position.

It had its bad moments of dealing with many types of people, but the financial gain made an individual endure the job. I also met interesting people while working as a cab driver. I had several clients who were particularly good with tips and they desired me as their regular driver. It is amazing how important a cab can be to people's life existence. My services were needed, and I was happy to give my clients accommodations.

Time seemed to pass quickly at the cab company. The 1980s were ending, and the job at the cab company continued to go well for me. I had many interesting clients from females to males. I once had a call to pick up a client in the city of Hawthorne, California.

The client requested to be picked up on a certain corner on the main street of the city. The client waved me down and I picked him up. The client had several bags in his hands and seemed to be in an extreme hurry. Little did I know that the bags in the client's procession were bags from a bank robbery.

As I drove toward the client's requested destination, I looked in my rear-view mirror and saw red and blue flashing lights. It was the Hawthorne Police Department with its sirens on. I was ordered to pull over, and I did. The police ordered everyone out of the cab and began to search the entire cab. They pulled out the rear seats of the cab and found the bags of money under the seats. I was detained by the Hawthorne Police for a lengthy time and was then released. It was really something to go through; witnessing a police arrest of a bank robber was a very traumatizing event.

There was never a dull moment at the cab company. I was busy every day and continued to make a particularly good salary daily. I now lived and worked in the city of Inglewood, California. I did not have a good relationship with the dispatcher at the cab company, but I put up with his behavior. I put up with his behavior because I desired to keep my job.

His name was John and he had a bad disposition toward me. I did nothing to offend him, but he still acted offensive toward me. I dealt with the situation to maintain my job. Another interesting event occurred at the cab company. I stopped at one of the local donut shops in Inglewood for a cup of coffee and donut. I often stopped there for moments of relaxation and conversation. My first cousin, named Herman Miles, would also stop there very often. My cousin grew up with me as a child in the state of Louisiana. We also grew up together in the city of Los Angeles, California. We were both used to the streets of Los Angeles and its way of life.

I saw him sitting at his usual table in the donut shop. The donut shop was called Winchell's. People met there to talk and discuss business and pleasurable topics. I saw my cousin Herman sitting with a group of people. I bought a cup of coffee and a donut and walked over to the table where my cousin was sitting. I took a seat across from the table where he was seated.

As I sat at my table, I noticed my cousin was sitting with an incredibly beautiful young lady. It was not his wife and they were having an enjoyable conversation. I listened to the conversation that my cousin and all the people were having. I finally made sense of what they were discussing and joined the conversation. I was not interested in what my cousin and the people were discussing, but in the young lady to whom my cousin was talking.

I sat there looking and listening to the entire group of people talk about different subjects. I was waiting for an opportunity to ask my cousin for an introduction to the pleasant lady at the table. I finally got my chance after the conversation at their table had gone down. I immediately asked my cousin to introduce me to the young lady. My cousin apologized to me and then introduced the young lady to me. Her name was Veronica. She said hello to me with such a delightful smile. Her voice was very charming and she carried herself in such a pleasing manner.

The conversation at the table continued and I continued to listen. It turned out that Veronica was a former employee of the donut shop, but was seeking employment elsewhere. Several people left the group and exited the coffee shop. My cousin and Veronica were still at the table and getting ready to depart. I overheard Veronica tell my cousin that she had to hurry to catch her bus home. This was my chance and opportunity to get to know Veronica in the future. I quickly said to her very politely, "Veronica, I have a cab outside." I told her that I would be incredibly happy to drive her to her house and charge her no cab fee.

Veronica hesitated, but eventually said yes to the offered cab ride. I was so glad that she did; it was a pleasure to talk and ride along with her. In the short distance from the coffee shop to where she lived, I found her company very pleasurable and I enjoyed being with her. As we came to her house, I quickly asked for her telephone number. Veronica hesitated, so I quickly gave her my number.

As she walked toward her house, I called out to her, "Call me." I did not go to that coffee shop that often, but I was glad I did on that day. Days and weeks went by, and I continued to work for the cab company. I would often think of my meeting with Veronica and hoped she would give me a phone call. I came home one evening and I was relaxing in my small apartment. My telephone rang and I picked it up. On the other end was Veronica; it was a pleasure to hear from her. I thought she was not going to give me a return call, but she did. I was overjoyed and made plans to see her once again. I asked her if she would like to have dinner with me and to take her to a movie. She told me she would like a dinner and a movie. I was incredibly happy that she said yes to our date. It was something I really anticipated.

I had several relationships before I met Veronica. One was with a woman named Cynthia M. She became pregnant during the relationship and a male child was born. Cynthia named the child Chance. I was not allowed to attend the child's birth. It would be years later that I would see the child after paying child support and having a suspended driver's license. Later on, the child would contact me for closure about his birth. I was not allowed to bond with the child, Chance, for years. This was due to the feelings that his mother held for me from my previous relationship with her. The misunderstandings and anger from the relationship caused her to retaliate against me. In later years, the child, Chance, would agree to a DNA test. The test came out 99 percent positive and gave closure to all parties involved.

Veronica and I enjoyed each other's company very much. The days turned into weeks, and the weeks turned into months. We discussed many things during our dating relationship. Veronica informed me that she was from the state of Louisiana. She had worked several jobs while in the Inglewood and the Los Angeles area. She had come to California from the state of Louisiana to better her career in general. She lived with her aunt in the central area of Los Angeles, California.

We often talked of the state of Louisiana. I was informed by Veronica that her father was acquainted with my uncle. Her father had known my uncle for many years and other relatives who lived near my uncle's hometown of Homer, Louisiana. It was utterly amazing that our relatives knew one another before our actual meeting. One might say it is, indeed, a small world.

We had a lot in common. We both desired similar things in life such as good jobs, nice living arrangements, and the good side of life.

It was the 1990s, and the world had changed. Men and women were living together prior to their marital status. Veronica and I discussed the things we both desired in life and the topic of marriage. I thought about marriage before, but now the opportunity presented itself to me. I found someone who I was comfortable with physically and mentally. I wanted to make sure I kept our relationship together, so I ask Veronica for her hand in marriage. Veronica accepted my proposal for marriage, and we were officially engaged. We both made plans for our wedding and better living arrangements.

I was still working at the cab company and the financial gain was still good. After my engagement with Veronica, I wanted her to meet my parents. I was incredibly happy to introduce Veronica to my parents. Even though my dad was ill with colon cancer, he and my mother welcomed Veronica with open arms. My sisters were also there, and they, too, welcomed Veronica to the family. Everyone in my family was glad I was finally getting married.

I kept working at the cab company and Veronica was working in the city of Inglewood at the senior citizen's home as a guest attendant representative. We both enjoyed our time while living in the city of Inglewood. We had considered moving into a larger dwelling than our small apartment. Our plans for our wedding seemed to coincide with the plans for our new living arrangements.

My parents acquired a property next door to their house and were renting the houses out as rental property. The people renting the front house were moving out and it was available for rental. This was just right for Veronica and I with regard to our plans for a larger living area. We discussed the subject with my parents and decided to accept the new housing. We looked at the front house and liked it very much. The house was extremely larger than the place we had in Inglewood. The rent was quite suitable and the area was not that bad at the time.

My fiancé and I were overjoyed to acquire the house and the new living accommodations. My father was becoming more ill from his medical condition. Cancer and other underlying conditions had severely damaged his body. My father's illness was exceedingly difficult for me and the rest of my family to endure. We were used to seeing him up and around and full of energy. It was not the same to see him so ill and not doing the things he loved to do.

After viewing the house next door to my mother's house, it was time for Veronica and I to make the trip back to the west side of Los Angeles, California. My mother was worried about our safety going back to the apartment. The Rodney King riots were going on in Los Angeles and the California National Guard patrolled the streets. Veronica and I were terrified to see the fire and destruction within the Los Angeles area. We made it to our destination, but not without trauma. The year 1992 was a happy and sad year, for both of us. My upcoming marriage to Veronica was a happy occasion, but my father's illness weighed heavily on both of us.

A brief time before Veronica and I were supposed to move into the house next door to my parents, my father succumbed to his illness; it was an extremely sad time in the family. I was so happy to have Veronica at my side during that time. Nothing could take away the pain from the loss of my father, but Veronica's presence helped to make my loss more bearable. It seemed that everything was in alignment. The death of my father left my mother alone, and I was able to comfort her in her time of need by moving next door to her.

Meeting Veronica at the time that I did allowed me to have her at my side and support me. These things seemed to occur not by chance, but by fate. Once again, I thought about my old friend *destiny*. We moved into our new place of residence and began to build our future with each other. I was still with the cab company and making ends meet. The days and months passed by, and many things occurred for the better.

We spoke with Veronica's uncle who was a minister. He agreed to marry us in his church and gave us his blessings. We set our wedding date for the month of August. As we got ourselves ready for our wedding, we became even closer in spiritual content and emotions. My mother was adapting to the loss of my father and was happy for Veronica and I getting married. Families on both sides welcomed our wedding. Veronica's parents made plans to attend our wedding and gave their blessings. We were about to become spouses, and we both had anticipated it very much. I often dreamed about marriage, and now marriage was becoming a reality.

The years of the nineties were full of different things for me and Veronica. We had been together for a considerable time while dating and developed a good understanding of each other. We discussed topics of material things we desired and of familyhood. Marriage is, indeed, a unique way of life for any individual to experience. Being single and then getting married is an incredibly challenging occurrence for any individual. A person must be able to accept the fact that they are no longer alone, and complete sharing is a mandatory event. An individual must be able to look upon their mate with the same feelings as they have for themselves. There is no time to practice individualism in any marriage. Sharing with your mate should start early in any relationship. I believe that dating and living together prior to marriage is a good procedure. Both individuals get to know each other in many ways. Each person gets to observe each other's habits and their good and bad sides. This is, indeed, vital to the survival of any marriage.

The time for our wedding was quickly approaching. Veronica and I, as well as our entire families, were busy deciding things toward our wedding. Things had to be done like ordering the wedding cake, wedding garments, hair grooming, many rehearsals for the wedding, and wedding reception. It was a time of pleasure and a great deal of work for everyone involved. The day finally came for our wedding and I was happy in every way, but extremely sad that my dad could not be there to witness my marriage.

It was now 1992, and many things occurred in my life: the death of my beloved father and meeting Veronica. Both happy and sad things occurred, but that is definitely a part of life's cycle. Our wedding was held in the lower main area of Los Angeles, California. The wedding went as planned; it, indeed, was a beautiful event. Minister Robert Kimble was the presiding minister. He was Veronica's uncle, and he allowed the use of his church to marry us.

We were church members and knew the members of the church. The church was named Mount Beulah Missionary Baptist Church and was a small church of considerable size. After Veronica reached the altar joined by her father, the ceremony started with me singing a song to Veronica. The song was called "A One in a Million You." It fit the mood of the occurring event and I enjoyed singing it to Veronica.

After the vows were read, the pastor pronounced us as husband and wife. As the ceremony ended in the church, different wedding guests and several members of our church congratulated us. A limousine awaited us outside of the church to take us to the wedding reception. The wedding reception was being held at Veronica's aunt's home. Her name was Dorothy, but family members called her by the nickname "Dolly." She was a pleasant person and looked upon Veronica as a daughter. She and her husband, Bob, had a beautiful home around Windsor Hills, California. It was a very exclusive area mixed with various races and considered to be a high-end area for real estate.

The wedding reception went exceptionally well, and everyone had a joyous time. There were plenty of delicious food and beverages for our wedding guests. It had a very joyous atmosphere, filled with laughter and conversations. Veronica and I were happy for ourselves and thankful to them for their beautiful wedding gifts. The wedding gifts given to us filled our home with various things we needed. We had to buy extraordinarily few items when it came to utensils, bedding covers and sheets, and several other household objects.

The reception lasted for several hours and was continuously joyful up to the ending hour. We thanked the relatives of Veronica for the use of their home. We then started to pack all our wedding gifts in the limousine. A close friend of mine, named Charley, helped us with the various packages. Charley worked at the same cab company as me and always had my back. We departed the reception area and headed home. We both thanked my friend, Charley, as he helped us unpack our wedding gifts. We then entered our house as Mr. and Mrs. Hill.

As I lifted Veronica through the front door of the house, I felt a true moment of completion toward fulfilling my obligations as a man. I had taken my wedding vows very seriously upon my marriage to Veronica. I realized that these vows were ordained and meant not to be broken. They were vows that were taken by people for centuries. They were vows to honor each other for better or worse or till death do us part. They were also vows that the Almighty God ordained for marriage between a man and a woman.

Veronica and I were busy with housekeeping and things in general that newlyweds do. We were both working, and our combined incomes helped meet our bills. I was still working at the cab company and making a suitable salary. Sometimes I would have over two hundred dollars in my personal possession. I made this amount of money many times before in one day.

One day, I was taking a break from my regular driving duties and stopped at a small neighborhood store. I stopped to get something to drink and a pack of cigarettes. As I made my way to the store, I saw three young black men sitting in front of the store. One of them said hello and the others looked at me as I entered the door. I purchased the things that I needed and made my exit from the store.

As I walked to the cab, I felt an arm encircling my neck. It was a horrifying feeling and absolutely breathtaking. I felt as though my breath had been taken away. The larger one of the trio held me in a chokehold, and the other two began hitting me in several areas of my body. I could not fight off my assailants and was beaten very badly. My lip was busted and several parts of my body were in extreme pain from the beating. All the money that I made that day had been taken by my assailants. As the three criminals made their getaway, I made my way back to the cab. I picked up a small handgun that I carried for my personal protection. I looked down the street and saw the three robbers running away. They were in line with my gun to fire. I had a choice to fire my gun at them or let them escape into the populated area. I made the choice to let them go without firing my weapon. I was terribly upset about my injuries and the day's proceeds of money.

It was a good thing I did not fire that gun in the heavily populated area. The Inglewood Police informed me about the consequences of striking someone else other than the suspects. The police informed me that I could have been charged if the bullet from my gun hit an innocent bystander. I was glad that I did not fire that weapon as angry as I was. After the police made and took their complete criminal report, I headed back to the Inglewood Cab Company. I was asked about the cab robbery and filled out the daily report and was released for the day. Later, I had to go to the doctor to receive medical treatment for my injuries. I had to receive several stitches to my lip area and several x-rays of my body. The cab company paid all, and I was given time off by the owner of the Inglewood Cab Company.

I had been married for a good year or more, it was a tough time for such a thing to occur. Veronica was terribly upset about the cab robbery and my injuries more so. We discussed the possibility of finding a safer job and a change of career. Veronica was right about the dangers of the job and was already considering making a change in career. As I healed up at home, I started to search for jobs at the same time. The money I made at the cab company had been good in the past years but had begun to decrease in flow. The decision to change jobs was in the making prior to the cab robbery. I was considering that change because of my marriage and plans for a family.

After healing from the injuries I got from the cab company, I submitted my resignation. The company had been a reliable source of income for several years. It was now time to move on to other job opportunities. I searched for various job openings in fields related to my job experience. A temporary employment agency called the Professional Temporary Agency found various jobs for individuals in their related fields. It was a very prestigious agency and referred me to several excellent job assignments.

I was also still working in the field of acting, and the background work in movies was exceptionally good. The jobs in the movies paid about eighty dollars a day, and that was good money if you were called by the casting agency for a movie role. I was involved with jobs in movie background work on a regular basis. Financially, it was working out to a degree of financial survival.

Veronica, in her earlier years, had attended school that prepared individuals for the career in economic management and banking. She had worked several temporary agency jobs and finally got hired by one of the largest banking firms in the state of California at that time in the 1990s. She made exceptionally good money while working for the bank and loved her job very much. We had now been married for several years and doing good for newlyweds.

One evening, we both returned home from our daily activities. Veronica had been having various issues with her appetite and feeling not her usual self at times. She requested to see an obstetrician for an overall examination. We made an appointment to see an obstetrician, and she was examined by the doctor thoroughly. The doctor told us to wait for the results of the examination and that they would be ready in a few days.

Those days of waiting seemed to last an exceptionally long time, and we continually wondered about the results. The day finally came and the pregnancy test results returned. We were told by the attending physician that the test was positive. It was a moment of excitement and joy for both of us and the obstetrician as well. We immediately began to make plans to inform our families on both sides. We also realized that things were going to be different for us in many ways. Having a baby would be a new way of life for us. It was something that we both wanted and were thankful for God to receive.

We both had been through relationships that did not work out. We both were also raised in families with a good Christian religion that welcomed children. When a man's wife becomes pregnant, it tends to change the father in several ways. It gave me a more complete feeling about myself and strengthened my feelings toward life. We both continued to work on our jobs and prepared for the birth of our child. Veronica was given the option of continuing to work on her job or take parental leave. Veronica was making an exceptionally good salary and decided to continue working. The bank that she worked with was considerate to her in many ways during her pregnancy. She was happy and content while working during her pregnancy. The bank also gave us a baby shower in celebration of our child's birth. It was a beautiful and well-organized event. It reminded me of our wedding reception and the different gifts we received for our house. The only difference was the type of gifts; this time, they were baby attire.

We enjoyed the baby shower immensely and the companionship of Veronica's coworkers as well. Veronica's coworkers knew we were having a male child and purchased baby boy attire. We returned home and marveled over the baby gifts that we received from the bank employees. The days continued, and Veronica continued to work at her job.

Her uncle was the pastor of the church where we got married. The pastor was worried about her working during her pregnancy. He suggested that Veronica take an early parental leave several times. As the time for the birth approached, I was also concerned about Veronica's working schedule. Our obstetrician examined Veronica and informed us that he was requesting an early parental leave. The request from our obstetrician was forwarded to Veronica's job, and she was placed on an early parental leave. The time of birth for our child was supposed to be on August 8, 1995. Veronica had been placed on parental leave about a month and a half before her due date. We stayed close to the house and made sure that Veronica was comfortable.

We were taking Lamaze classes and seeing our obstetrician on a constant basis. Veronica's mother made the trip from the state of Louisiana and was staying with us. It gave Veronica and I a comfortable feeling to have her nearby. As the month of July continued to pass, we thought of our child's birth date in August 1995. We continued to attend the Lamaze classes and monitor Veronica's every move.

One evening we were preparing to go to a Lamaze class. Veronica was taking a shower and said she felt a strange feeling come down her leg while showering. She said she would mention it to the instructor at the Lamaze class. We got used to the regular routine of attending the classes. As we sat in the class during our regular Lamaze exercises, Veronica mentioned the incident in the shower to an instructor. The instructor told us that Veronica's water broke and she had to quickly go to the labor delivery, recovery, and postpartum room.

We were totally surprised to find out that our child was going to be born earlier than expected. It was a blessing for us to be attending the Lamaze class while Veronica's water broke. When a woman's water breaks, it is time for a woman to give birth. It was a time of thankfulness and joy for the upcoming birth of our son. It was also a blessing for us to be in the hospital shortly after her water broke; we did not have to rush through traffic to the hospital.

It seemed like a long night for me and all involved. The months of anticipation had ended, and the reality of me being a father was finally at hand. We decided to name my son after my father's name and my name. His name would be Elbert Evan Hill III. Veronica was in the delivery room, and I paced the floor of the delivery room. Several hours passed, and the attending Dr. Noel gave me the joyful news of my son's birth. Our son was born a healthy Black male with no underlying medical issues. That moment was more than magnificent; it was a divine feeling of joy and satisfaction. Of all the things that occur on this earth, the birth of a child to a parent is truly one of the most glorifying events to be stored upon a man and woman. We were the parents of a six-pound–four-ounce baby boy.

All went well during the delivery of our child. Veronica had some difficulty with delivery pains, but they were normal for a normal baby's birth. Veronica delivered our baby, and our child was taken to the hospital nursery. I watched our baby boy as he lay in the hospital nursery. The sight of seeing my son kicking and crying was one that pleased me in every way. So much can happen during childbirth other than having normal childbirth. We were blessed that Veronica made it through the delivery, and we had a beautiful bundle of joy to take home.

After several hours of observation by the delivery doctor, Veronica was released to return home. It had been a long night, and we were glad to return home. Veronica's mother was overjoyed and glad to see her grandbaby. All the way home, the car was full of joyful conversation about our baby boy. It was a moment we had dreamed of for nine months during Veronica's pregnancy. Many thoughts ran through my mind about the birth of my son. I thought of my new responsibilities as a parent and father. I thought of the deaths of my father and the death of Veronica's uncle. My father passed away before our son's birth, and so did Veronica's uncle. I thought of how happy they would have been to see the baby. They were both so extremely helpful and loving when it came to family matters. They gave us a great deal of support toward building our marriage and family as well.

Veronica's mother stayed with us for several weeks after the delivery of our child. She was enjoying the presence of the new baby and being a grandmother. As the days and weeks passed, it came time for Veronica's mother to return home to Louisiana. She had really enjoyed her trip, and the birth of her grandson even more so. After the departure of Veronica's mother, we were busy with parenting duties. It was truly a new experience for both Veronica andI. We both had been around other people's children before, but now, we had our own responsibility of raising a child. It felt great being a father and Veronica enjoyed being a mother also.

We were getting used to parenthood and the responsibilities that came with it. After several weeks of recuperation from her hospital delivery, Veronica went back to work. She was glad to return to work and mingle with her coworkers. I was working in the movies as a background actor and working various temporary jobs as well. When I was not on job assignments or working the background in movies, I stayed at home with our baby. Most of the time, Veronica's auntie watched our baby while we were at work. Her Aunt Rodesa was a godsend and was always there for us. She was faithful to us for years with her loving care of babysitting our son. We had nothing to worry about while we were away from our son.

The days of the 1990s passed abruptly. Our son was growing up at an extremely fast pace and learning his basic motor skills. It is amazing how quickly a baby can grow from infancy to becoming a toddler. We were overjoyed to watch our child grow up and develop into a strong and healthy child.

The climate for the job market in the state of California was veritable. Major companies were either closing or merging with other major companies. The merging of banks took place on a large scale during the late 1990s. Veronica's bank was one of the Californian banks that merged with another bank. These merges often caused employees to be misplaced and caused a loss of employment. This happened to Veronica's bank, and she lost her position at her old bank.

It was a very disappointing time for us financially to lose that amount of income. I was still working in the background for movies and my temporary job assignments. It was tough going financially, but we managed to hold things together. Veronica decided to sign up with various temporary agencies and joined the acting agency as well. With those temporary jobs and the background movie assignments, we manage to take care of our bills and family. I filled out applications at different employment agencies. I was seeking a job with higher pay and better health insurance.

During the late nineties, I decided to join the Veterans of Foreign Wars. It was an organization for ex-military veterans with combat disabilities. It was close to our house and I enjoyed going to the annual meetings. Veronica also joined the women's auxiliary. The post and its members were very hospitable to my wife and I. We attended several events given by the post commander and its members. They were always filled with fun and we had plenty of good eating. The Veterans of Foreign Wars was an extremely good outlet for my wife andI. My post commander wanted to give a benefit dinner sponsored by our post. It was approved by the members of the post and scheduled to be held at the Patriotic Hall in the city of Los Angeles, California.

The Patriotic Hall was one of the most beautiful ballrooms in the heart of the downtown Los Angeles area. Its ballrooms were filled with magnificent art effects and beautiful decors. All the post members were expected to sell tickets to the upcoming event by our post. My job was to sell as many tickets as I could and sing the national anthem. The selling of tickets was not easy, but we managed to sell all the printed tickets to the military event.

The day of the event finally arrived, and we were ready for the show. My wife and I arrived at Patriotic Hall and hundreds of cars packed the parking lot. They were people who came to view the beautiful Patriotic Hall and have dinner and mingle. At these events, people networked and shared various bits of vital information in reference to veterans' rights and related information. The commander of our post opened the event with a military welcome to the various military auxiliary in attendance. The commander then introduced me to the stage to sing the national anthem.

I walked on the stage, approached the microphone, and introduced myself to the audience. I was going to sing the national anthem with no background music. It was very well received by the entire audience within the ballroom. As I finished the song, I received a standing ovation from the audience. A feeling of pride and satisfaction surrounded me completely. I felt as though a brick wall had been lifted off my shoulders. I felt that way because many of the California auxiliaries were in attendance. It meant a lot to our post that the presentation of the song was given accordingly.

While attending the meetings at the Veterans of Foreign Wars, I received a letter from the United States Postal Service. The letter stated that my application had been accepted, and I was scheduled for an interview. I went to the interview and passed all the entry-level examinations for my job category. I passed the examinations for a custodial position in the maintenance department of the postal service. It was a blessed event to happen to me. I needed the federal job at the post office to better support my family and myself.

The 1990s were ending, and the turn of the century was approaching. The years passed, bringing about many changes in the lives of my family. Veronica and I had been married for several years, and our son, Trey, was growing up rapidly. The years had passed from the time of our son's birth until the turn of the century. Many different things occurred from the early 1960s to the turn of the century in 1999. I survived a war, readjusted to being home again, attended college, and made graduation. My marriage to Veronica and the birth of our son were major turning points for me as a man and as a disabled veteran.

My wife had given me a great deal of inspiration in applying for a higher disability rating from the Veterans Admiration. I had delayed my request for a higher level of disability. My wife's constant reminders of my wounds from combat sent me on a new campaign to claim a higher disability rate. I followed through with the request to the Veterans Administration for a higher disability. It took a lengthy time, but the Department of Veterans Affairs finally met my request.

I was given close to a 100 percent rating by the Department of Veterans Affairs. The new rating from the Veterans Administration was a significant help financially. Veronica was able to spend more time with our son and refrain from working if she chose to do so.

We had been blessed many times over by God in every way. All the things that I spoke of throughout my life story, I had dreamed of them prior to their occurrence. Some people might say certain things that happen were a coincidence or chance. I cannot justly make such conclusions about the events of my life. Without any doubt, I could say it was destiny as the contributing factor to my life course.

After many life experiences, I am convinced of destiny's force and presence. Be your own judge of the accepted definition of the word *destiny*. What is meant to be will be. What is not meant to be will not be. From the days of my youth till the days of my young adulthood, I often wondered about the occurrences in my younger life. I did not comprehend the presence of destiny in my life on a daily basis. As I grew older, I begin to comprehend destiny's meaning. Everyone must live and experience life—to accept or not accept the existence of destiny in their life.

CONCLUSION

I want to place special emphasis on the topic of returning veterans from different wars. Many people have asked me my feelings about the topic. I will always view America as the leader in the democratic way of life. I have certain political views concerning the treatment of veterans by the honorable government after military release. I feel that most returning veterans are not taken care of properly, especially those who return home with serious wounds sustained from combat in a foreign war.

Being a disabled veteran myself, I can give a firsthand view of the undertreatment of some returning veterans. War itself is hell, in every sense, and has truly little mercy on the defeated or the victorious. Upon my return home, I was uncertain about getting disability compensation from the Veterans Administration. Moments of uncertainty in reference to my compensation from the federal government in relationship to service-connected disabilities. I had to constantly battle with the Veterans Administration for injury compensation. The returning veterans of Vietnam were not treated very nicely by the American society in general.

The vast majority looked upon the veterans of Vietnam as automatically having some type of mental problem. This was true in many cases, but all veterans deserved a chance to readjust themselves upon their homecoming. It was an extremely challenging time in my life, as well as thousands of my fellow veterans' lives. We had been placed in a difficult situation. Many veterans were killed on the streets in many different cities. This was due to the neglect and disregard of the medical care which was desperately needed by individual veterans.

Some parents of returning veterans did not have the patience to deal with returning veterans, and the outcome was disastrous. I was truly fortunate to have patient and understanding parents. My parents were there for me whenever I needed their support. The aftermath of war can be just as challenging as the frontline of combat. The return of a soldier to their home is, indeed, a challenge. Male or female, they will face reconditioning from every source. The challenge becomes more challenging for the veterans who were wounded or who received PTSD or stages of other related traumatic conditions. From the conditions of PTSD comes extreme depression, and it interferes with the daily life of the veteran.

The war in Vietnam caused thousands of post-traumatic stress disorder. These problems and other medical problems acquired by any veteran should be addressed on an immediate basis. The sacrifices made by all veterans should not go unrewarded. The willingness to give their lives for the safety and preservation of their nation speaks for itself.

I made the decision to go to war and accepted my fate. I survived the Vietnam War and my reentry into American society successfully. I am thankful for the opportunity to tell my story. When it comes the time for destiny to end my life, let it be said by all who witness the event. "There lies a Black man who not only lived in America, but also there lies a man called Patriot Hill."

In my later years, I had to retire from the United States Postal Service. The postal service had been good to me in many ways. The annual salary was extraordinarily good, and there was always room for job advancement. I started out as a custodian in the maintenance department of the post office, but went on to become an electronic repair technician. I had taken several battery tests and passed them to become a G4-level electronic technician.

I really advanced in the postal service during my first year. I advanced in pay level, as well as in my grade level with the post office. As an electronic technician, I had to utilize my hands and fingers on an everyday basis. The job assignments were very demanding when it came to using the hands and fingers. There were daily repairs, which required a great deal of hand and finger motion usage.

I was an electrical repair man for many years with the postal service. Eventually, the continued usage of my hands and fingers created a weakness in my hands.

The everyday turning of a screwdriver and the gripping of other tools had given me a condition called the carpal tunnel. It was a condition where the nerves and the bones of the fingers were worn down because of torque usage of the hands. It got to the point that my hands would be in pain if I utilized them too much. My private doctor examined my hands and told me I had a severe case of carpal tunnel. He asked me how long I had been working with my hands in their present condition. I informed him that I had been working with my hands for quite some time. The doctor then informed me that if I continued to work with my hands, I would eventually lose control of my hands.

I was informed that I could not do the same job anymore at the post office. The attending doctor was named Dr. Brigham, and I was thankful for his diagnosis. The doctor wrote a letter to the post office about my medical condition. The letter stated that I could not use my hands any longer in the same capacity. He ordered that I be given lighter duty and placed in better surroundings.

The year was 2003, and my regular duties were changed. I continued to work on light duty for several months after the diagnosis from my doctor. It was not easy dealing with the supervisors at my post office. I was often approached about retiring because of my medical condition. I had to seek help from the postal union on several occasions to defend my job status. It was not easy to contain myself in a job where I was humiliated on many occasions. I put in several years with the United States Postal Service. They had been good years for me and my family. I was placed on total disability by my doctor and the Department of Labor. It was time for me to consider complete retirement from the United States Postal Service.

In 2005, my retirement papers from the postal service were submitted to the post office personnel office. My wife and I made plans to leave the state of California prior to my retirement from the postal service. We decided to relocate to the state of Texas. We felt it would be better for our son's growing up and for our well-being as well. The property in the state of Texas in early 2000 was extremely agreeable. After dealing with the postal service in California for several months, I finally received my orders for retirement.

My wife and son had traveled to the state of Texas to view homes. We had been communicating from state to state about different homes in Texas. Before my retirement, we looked at several homes and were considering one that we liked out of the group. I was busy clearing the paperwork for my retirement. At the same time, my wife and son were in Texas purchasing our new home. It was an extremely busy time for us and we were busy with all kinds of legal matters. With all the extreme pressure placed upon us, we managed to complete our designated tasks. It finally came the time for me to join my family in Texas. It saddened me to leave my mother and niece in California, but joy came over me from the thought of rejoining my wife and son in Texas.

I had elected to drive to the state of Texas from the state of California. The drive took about eighteen hours, give or take. I arrived in Texas in the month of September 2006. My wife had already prepared the house with beautiful furniture and took care of our son's educational needs. Veronica truly held our new home together prior to my arrival in Texas. I missed my family very much during our transition to Texas. It was especially difficult for my son; he was only nine years old at the time. We endured the times of loneliness and finally were rejoined in the year 2006 in the state of Texas.

It is a terrible thing when a family must be separated under any conditions. I have now been a resident of Texas since 2006. I can truly say that I am a Texan indeed. I often think about many things in the past that have affected my life. Some of the things were good, and some of the things were bad. In closing my story, as a veteran of the Vietnam War, I must bring up the term *destiny* once again. I am convinced that *destiny* has taken its course in my life on a regular basis.

ABOUT THE AUTHOR

Elbert Hill Jr. has always had a love for his country. He volunteered for the United States Army. While serving in the army, he did a tour of duty in Vietnam. He received a Purple Heart medal for his wounds received in combat. He wishes to salute all veterans of various wars. He chose to make the ultimate sacrifice, in defending the democratic way of life.

P.S. Thank you for your service.